Presented to

_____

By

_____

Date

_____

SEEING
Christmas

by Karen Stacy

illustrated by Joel Schoon-Tanis

For my kids and grandkids—my inspiration, motivation, and encouragement.
Thank you for giving my poem its wings.

Printed in P.R.C.
First Printing, 2019
ISBN 978-1-5323-0102-5
Little Bird Press | Grand Rapids, MI 49301
Cover Design by Laura J. McDonald
Designed by 2 Fish Company

Dear Reader,

Years ago, I became frustrated hearing people say that Christmas is too materialistic.
I felt bombarded by all kinds of negative mindsets regarding its commercialism.

My mind and heart have always leaned toward the beauty of the Christmas season,
and I feel that God is in every detail of it. So I ventured to write a poem expressing to
my family how I *see* Christmas, hoping they might come to envision it similarly.
With much encouragement from them, that poem has become this book.

My prayer for you is that this little book will inspire a change in your perspective as well,
and that your Christmas experience would be more meaningful than ever before
because of it, this year and for many years to come.

Here's to *seeing* Christmas!
Tons of love, Karen

"The question is not what you look at, but what you see."
— Henry David Thoreau

It's that time of year!

Are you ready to see?
Come take a look
At Christmas with me...

The tree!
The tree!

With all of the ornaments,
Tradition and memories
Bring so much enjoyment.

The lights!
The lights!

They sparkle and shine,
Filling the room
With beauty divine.

The village!
The village!

It stands all aglow,
Lit up and covered
In a blanket of snow.

But WAIT!

Is this what Christmas is all about?
Some say no, but I want to shout!

YES, IT IS!

So perfectly!
And here is what I hope you'll see...

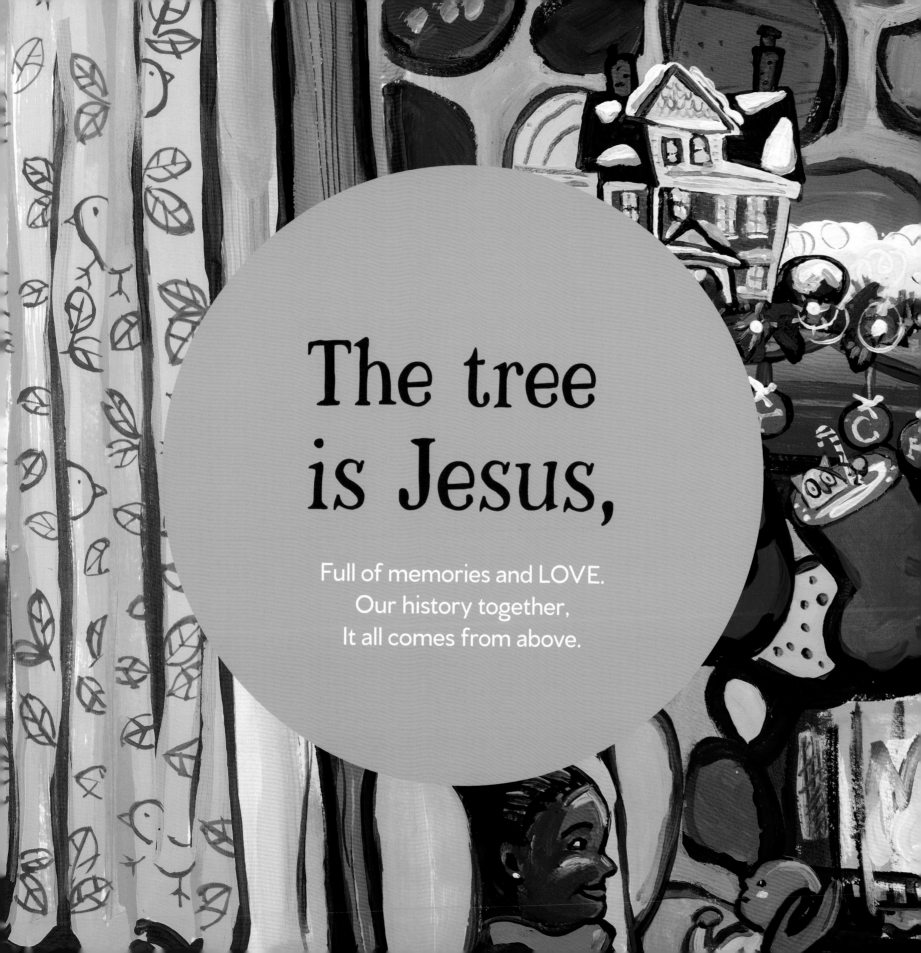

The tree is Jesus,

Full of memories and LOVE.
Our history together,
It all comes from above.

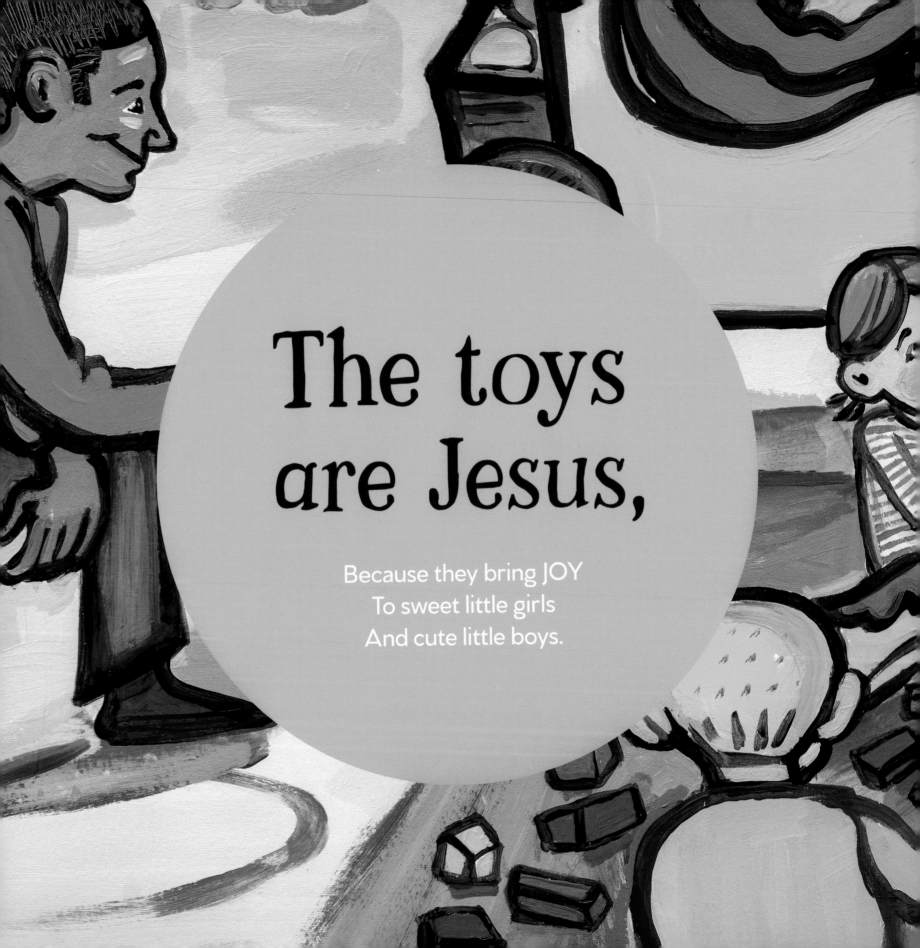

The toys are Jesus,

Because they bring JOY
To sweet little girls
And cute little boys.

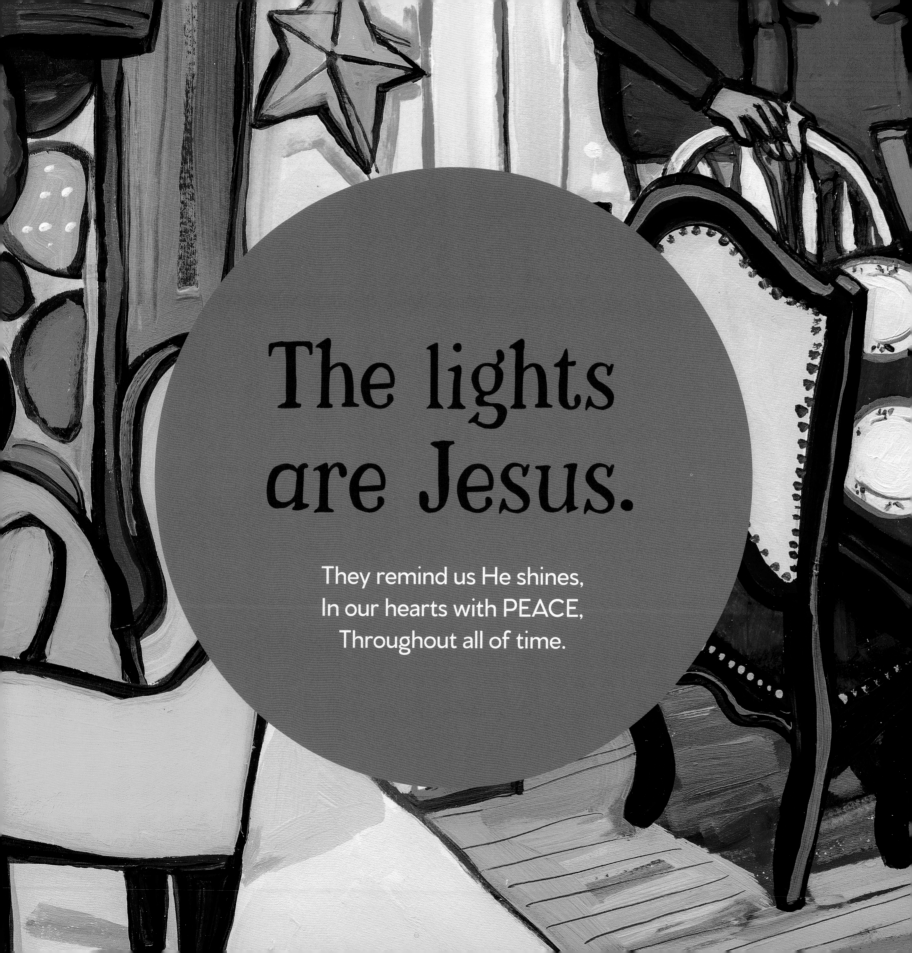

The lights are Jesus.

They remind us He shines,
In our hearts with PEACE,
Throughout all of time.

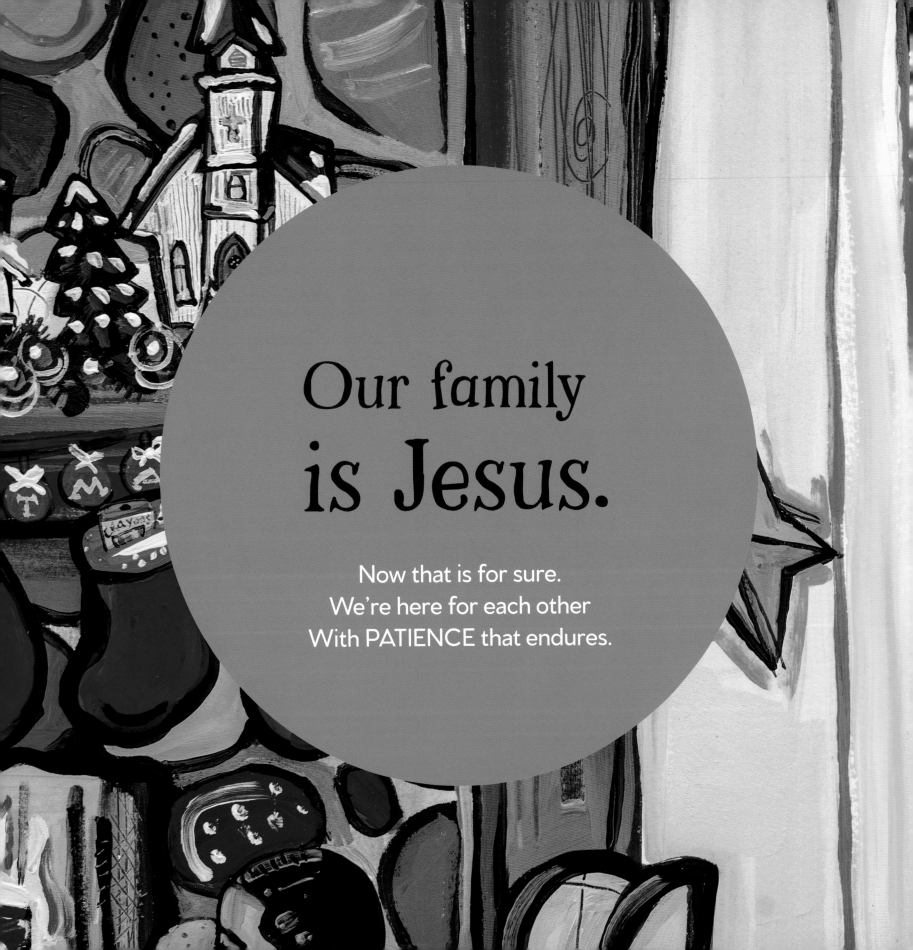

Our family is Jesus.

Now that is for sure.
We're here for each other
With PATIENCE that endures.

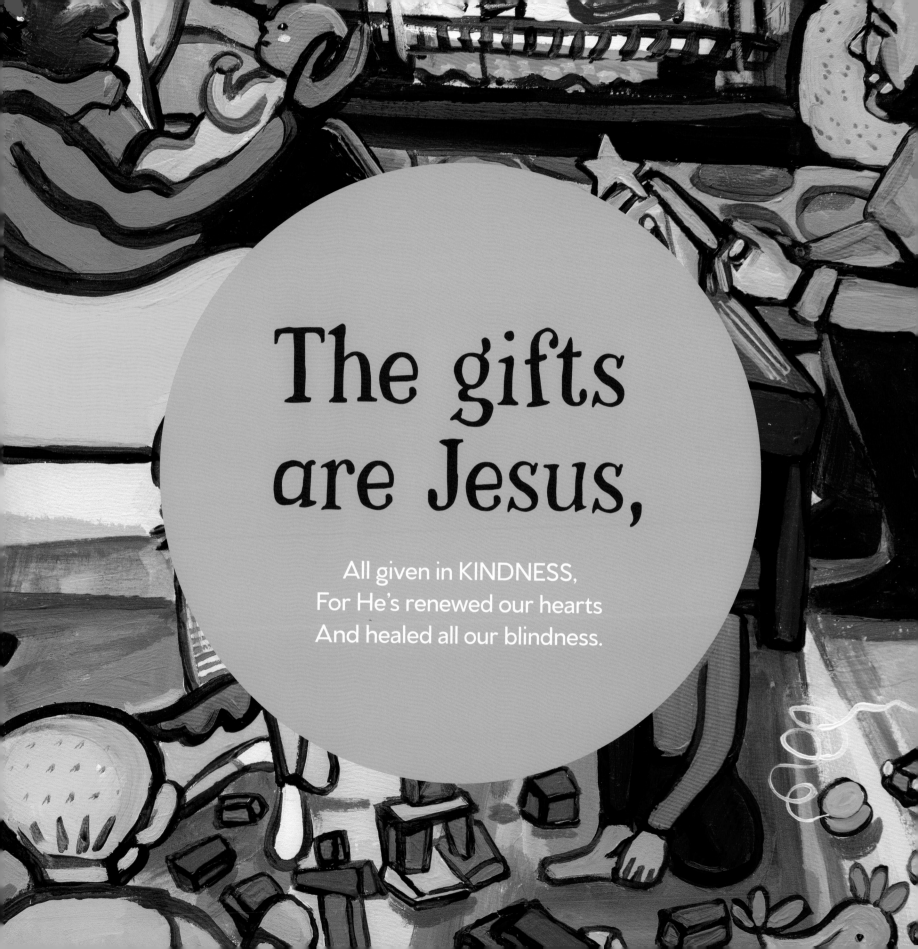

The gifts
are Jesus,

All given in KINDNESS,
For He's renewed our hearts
And healed all our blindness.

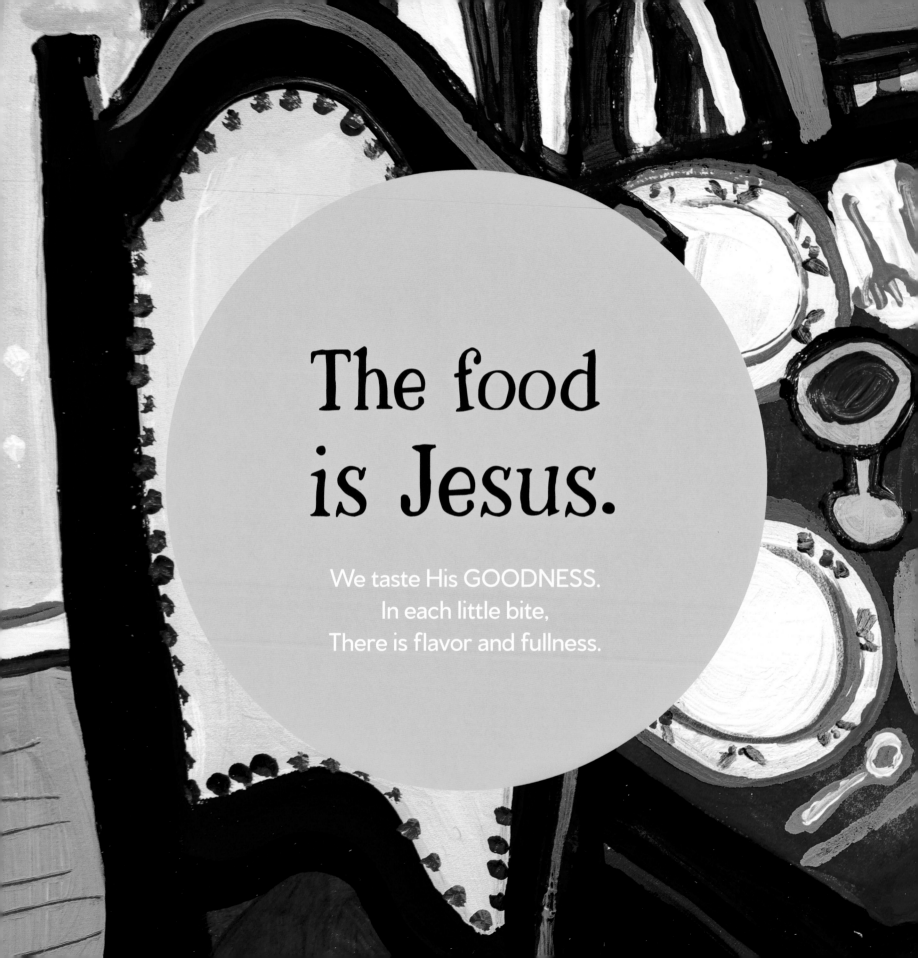

The food is Jesus.

We taste His GOODNESS.
In each little bite,
There is flavor and fullness.

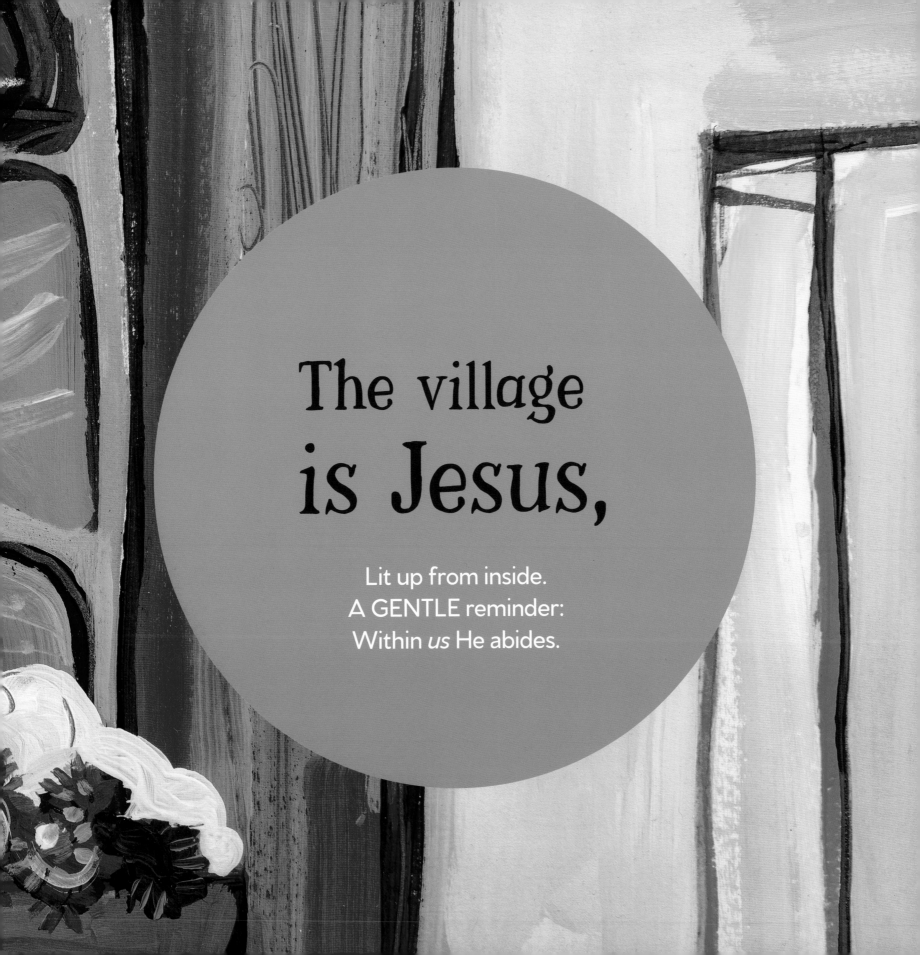

The village
is Jesus,

Lit up from inside.
A GENTLE reminder:
Within *us* He abides.

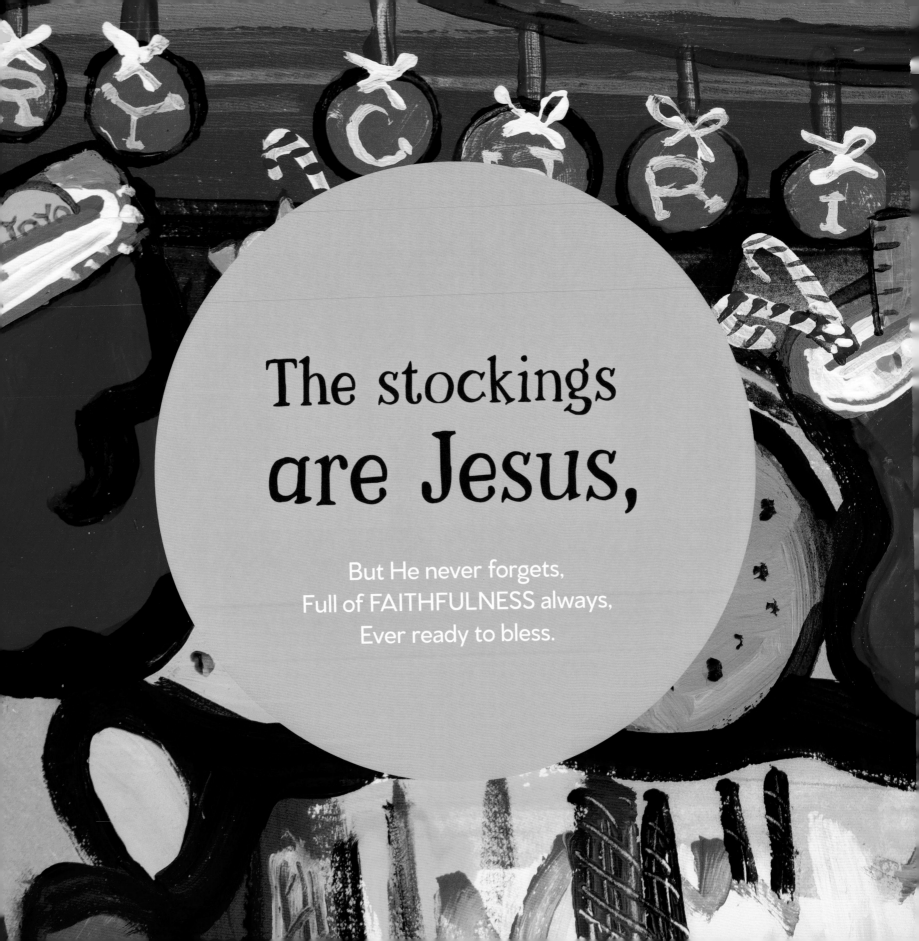

The stockings
are Jesus,

But He never forgets,
Full of FAITHFULNESS always,
Ever ready to bless.

So, you SEE... It's ALL JESUS!

He's everywhere!

If you look, you will find Him.

So be FULLY AWARE!

"The fruit of the Spirit is
love, joy, peace, patience, kindness, goodness,
faithfulness, gentleness, and self-control.
Against such things there is no law."

Galatians 5:22–23